Poptropica®

POPTOPICS · REAL WORLD FACTS

SPACE TRAVEL

by Tracey West

Poptropica
An Imprint of Penguin Group (USA) LLC

Special thanks to Buzz Aldrin

POPTROPICA
Published by the Penguin Group
Penguin Group (USA) LLC, 375 Hudson Street, New York, New York 10014, USA

USA | Canada | UK | Ireland | Australia | New Zealand | India | South Africa | China

penguin.com
A Penguin Random House Company

© 2007–2013 Pearson Education, Inc. All rights reserved. Published by Poptropica, an imprint of Penguin Group (USA) LLC, 345 Hudson Street, New York, New York 10014. Printed in the U.S.A.

ISBN 978-0-448-47794-7   10 9 8 7 6 5 4 3 2 1

Countdown to Liftoff . . . 10 . . . 9 . . . 8 . . .

Your heart pounds as the countdown reaches one. Your stomach lurches as your ship launches into the air, defying gravity to soar into the atmosphere . . . and beyond. Your ship rumbles as a passing asteroid glances it, sending you tumbling off course. Will you ever reach your destination?

In Poptropica, you can explore the stars and planets any time you want. You might safely land on the Moon, or get sucked into a black hole. Every visit is an adventure.

The space travels you take in Poptropica might seem like fantasy, but a lot of what you experience is based in reality. Sure, some of your Poptropica experiences might be beyond belief (space sharks, anyone?), but in this Poptropica book you'll discover that the universe is filled with things—real things—that are even more amazing.

Look for this symbol to see examples of how space travel has made its way into popular culture. **POP CULTURE**

This symbol will alert you to amazing facts about science. **POP SCIENCE**

Shoot for the Moon

A moon is a natural object in space that orbits another natural object in space, such as a planet. Moons can also orbit asteroids and stars. There are at least 171 moons in our solar system. The planet Jupiter alone has sixty-six! And Earth? Well, we've just got one.

We might be moon-deprived, but we humans are pretty obsessed with the one moon we have. For thousands of years, people have told stories about the Moon; worshipped it; and created beautiful paintings, songs, and poems about it. We have watched it through telescopes, and a few lucky humans have even walked on its surface.

In Poptropica, you can explore the moon, too, by joining a team of explorers living on a lunar colony.

What's in a Name?

The name of Earth's moon is the Moon (with a capital *M*). It's kind of like naming your dog Dog.

DOG ⟶

MOON

Welcome to the Moon

There's No Gift Shop, But It's Still Pretty Cool

If you made the 238,855-mile-long trip from Earth to the Moon, you'd have to wear a space suit if you wanted to step outside your ship once you got there. There are a few reasons for that. One is that the atmosphere on the moon is made up mostly of neon, hydrogen, helium, and argon—you'll need oxygen to breathe. The atmosphere is also a low-pressure one. This causes the gases in your body to expand, which would kill you pretty quickly, so your suit has to be pressurized.

Then there's the temperature, which can vary from sub–freezing cold (-388°F) to boiling hot (244°F). Your space suit would control the temperature to keep you comfortable (and alive).

The Man in the Moon

When you look up at a mostly full moon, you might think it resembles a face with two big, dark eyes. Humans have dubbed this face the "Man in the Moon." The "eyes" are actually dark basins called *maria*. They were formed when asteroids and other objects slammed into the Moon's surface, and then lava flowed in and hardened to fill the area. The area around the maria is called the highlands, which are marked with craters, mountains, and hills.

The Far Side of the Moon

No matter where you go on Earth, the Moon will always look the same. We are only able to see one side of the Moon, called the "near side." That's because of the way the Moon moves. It takes 29 days to orbit around Earth, and 29 days to completely rotate around its axis, so the "far side" is always just out of sight.

That doesn't mean no one has seen it. The Soviet Union's space probe *Luna 3* took photos of it in 1959, and astronauts of the Apollo 8 mission in 1968 flew past the far side and saw it with their own eyes. It consists mainly of highlands with fewer dark spots than the near side has.

Race to the Moon

Two Countries Face Off in a Space Race

Who will get to the Moon first? The Soviet Union or the United States? Follow the board to see who wins!

START

1957: THE SOVIETS LAUNCH SPUTNIK, A SATELLITE, INTO SPACE. IT'S THE FIRST MAN-MADE OBJECT TO BE PLACED IN EARTH'S ORBIT.

1958: THE US RESPONDS BY LAUNCHING A SATELLITE NAMED EXPLORER 1. THAT SAME YEAR, IT CREATES NASA, THE NATIONAL AERONAUTICS AND SPACE ADMINISTRATION.

1959: SOVIETS AIM THE FIRST PROBE, LUNA 2, AT THE MOON. IT'S A HIT!

1961: THE SOVIETS SEND COSMONAUT YURI GAGARIN INTO ORBIT, MAKING HIM THE FIRST HUMAN IN SPACE.

1961: ONE MONTH LATER, THE US SENDS ASTRONAUT ALAN SHEPARD INTO SPACE, BUT NOT INTO ORBIT.

WINNER: THE US, BY A FOOT (TWO FEET, ACTUALLY, AND THEY BOTH BELONGED TO NEIL ARMSTRONG).

FINISH

1969: SUCCESS! TWO US ASTRONAUTS—NEIL ARMSTRONG AND EDWIN "BUZZ" ALDRIN LAND ON THE MOON DURING THE APOLLO 11 MISSION. ARMSTRONG BECOMES THE FIRST HUMAN TO WALK ON THE MOON'S SURFACE.

1967: TRAGEDY STRIKES THE US SPACE PROGRAM WHEN THREE ASTRONAUTS ARE KILLED DURING A LAUNCH SIMULATION.

1968: NASA SENDS ASTRONAUTS INTO ORBIT AROUND THE MOON. THE US IS GETTING CLOSER TO ITS GOAL.

1963: SOVIET COSMONAUT VALENTINA TERESHKOVA BECOMES THE FIRST WOMAN IN SPACE, ORBITING EARTH 28 TIMES.

1962: THE US BEGINS PROJECT APOLLO, WITH THE GOAL OF LANDING A HUMAN ON THE MOON.

1961: LATER THAT MONTH, PRESIDENT JOHN F. KENNEDY PROMISES THAT THE US WILL "LAND A MAN ON THE MOON AND RETURN HIM SAFELY TO EARTH" BEFORE THE DECADE IS OVER.

1962: US ASTRONAUT JOHN GLENN GOES INTO ORBIT. THAT LEAVES ONE LAST FRONTIER: WHICH COUNTRY WILL SEND THE FIRST HUMAN TO THE MOON?

7

Anatomy of a Rocket

If you visit the Pewter Moon in Poptropica's Astro-Knights Island, you'll get to design a custom rocket ship that will take you further out into space. Here's a look at the real rocket, the *Apollo 11* space vehicle that took three American astronauts to the moon.

Apollo 11 was 363 feet tall. That's about as tall as a football field is long.

1. COMMAND MODULE: BIG ENOUGH TO HOLD THE THREE ASTRONAUTS, IT CONTAINED THE CONTROL CENTER—AND COUCHES—SO THE ASTRONAUTS COULD BE COMFORTABLE DURING THEIR THREE-DAY JOURNEY. MICHAEL COLLINS PILOTED THIS MODULE, WHICH WAS NAMED *COLUMBIA*.

2. SERVICE MODULE: THIS CONTAINED THE EQUIPMENT THAT HELPED STEER AND PROPEL THE CRAFT THROUGH SPACE. OXYGEN, HYDROGEN, AND FUEL WERE ALSO STORED HERE.

3. LUNAR MODULE: DUBBED *EAGLE*, THIS BROKE OFF FROM *APOLLO 11* AFTER THE ASTRONAUTS REACHED THE MOON'S ORBIT. NEIL ARMSTRONG PILOTED EAGLE AND BUZZ ALDRIN WENT WITH HIM. MICHAEL COLLINS STAYED BEHIND TO PILOT THE COMMAND MODULE.

4. LAUNCH VEHICLE: NAMED *SATURN V*, THIS PART OF THE *APOLLO 11* CRAFT LAUNCHED THE ROCKET INTO SPACE FROM ITS STARTING POINT IN WHAT IS NOW KNOWN AS CAPE CANAVERAL, FLORIDA. ITS SUPERCHARGED ROCKET ENGINES HAD TO ACCELERATE TO 25,000 MILES PER HOUR IN ORDER TO BREAK FREE FROM EARTH'S GRAVITY.

The first rocket ship was not imagined by a scientist, but by French author Jules Verne—way back in 1865. In his book *From the Earth to the Moon,* Verne tells the story of a "space cannon" that shoots a capsule containing three astronauts, who successfully reach the Moon.

POP CULTURE

POP SCIENCE

There was no bathroom on *Apollo 11.* Astronauts had to urinate into a hose that would send their urine into space.

On Poptropica's Lunar Colony, you can cruise the surface of the moon in a moon rover—just like the ones astronauts used on Earth's Moon.

Apollo LRVs

Why do you need a set of wheels on the Moon? Pretty much for the same reason we need them on Earth—to get around faster. Astronauts used Lunar Roving Vehicles on three space missions: Apollo 15, Apollo 16, and Apollo 17, allowing the astronauts to explore miles of the Moon's surface.

You can't just drive any vehicle on the Moon, though. They had to be specially made to travel across the Moon's bumpy terrain, and to operate in low gravity.

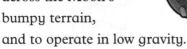

❑ ALUMINUM ALLOY FRAME

❑ SEAT BELTS

❑ ADJUSTABLE FOOTRESTS

❑ DISH ANTENNA (TRANSMITS TV SIGNALS TO EARTH)

❑ TITANIUM CHEVRONS ON TIRES PROVIDE TRACTION

❑ POWERED BY TWO 36-VOLT BATTERIES

A Used-Car Lot in Space

You won't be able to visit any of these LRVs in a museum. All three were left on the Moon.

POP CULTURE

A dune buggy is a vehicle that can travel across sandy terrain. It sort of resembles a lunar rover, so the LRVs got the nickname "Moon buggies."

Still in the Race

The Soviet Union didn't give up on space exploration after the US landed astronauts on the moon. In 1970, they sent the first LRV to the Moon. This one wasn't manned—it was robotic, making it officially the coolest remote-control vehicle in the galaxy.

Lunokhod 1 roamed the Moon for almost a year, taking readings of things such as radioactivity and cosmic radiation. *Lunokhod 2* went up in 1973 with improved navigation cameras. But the mission ended early when the rover tumbled into a crater. As a result, lunar dirt got on the radiator, causing the vehicle to overheat and die before its time.

Next Up, China!

In 2012, China announced plans to send an unmanned LRV to the Moon in 2013. The rover was named *Cheng'e 3*, after the Chinese moon goddess.

They've Gone Where Few Humans Have Gone Before

They're members of a pretty elite club. Between 1961 and 2011, 520 humans traveled into space. They came from thirty-eight different countries. Many of them were jet pilots; others were scientists, doctors, or engineers; and a few of them were just there to enjoy the view.

It takes a lot of talent to get into space (or at least a lot of cash), but you can go there anytime on Poptropica's Astro-Knights Island or Lunar Colony Island.

Which Naut Is Which?

Name	Country	Meaning
Astronaut	US	star (astro) + sailor (naut)
Cosmonaut	Soviet Union	universe (cosmo) + sailor (naut)
Taikonaut	China	space (taiko) + sailor (naut)

Suit up!

You can't be an astronaut without a space suit. Some of the main features of a modern space suit include:

Maximum Absorption Garment (MAG)—to collect the astronaut's urine (because there are no rest stops in space).

In-Suit Drink Bag (IDB) holds drinking water for the astronaut. (And if you drink too much, well, there's always the MAG . . .)

Primary Life Support Subsystem (PLSS) provides oxygen; controls the temperature; includes radio equipment and a warning system; and removes carbon dioxide exhaled by the astronaut.

Extravehicular Visor Assembly (EVA) protects the astronaut from bright sunlight (because sunglasses just won't fit over the helmet).

When you're on Earth, your spine is compressed by gravity. But in space, the spine expands and becomes longer. Astronauts can gain up to two inches in height while they are in space!

POP
SCIENCE

Space Travel Hall of Fame

ONCE AROUND THE PLANET

YURI GAGARIN, SOVIET UNION

FIRST HUMAN IN SPACE

ON APRIL 12, 1961, HE ORBITED EARTH ONCE IN THE *VOSTOK 1* SPACECRAFT. THE SON OF A CARPENTER, HE JOINED THE SOVIET AIR FORCE BEFORE BECOMING A COSMONAUT.

UP, UP, AND AWAY

ALAN SHEPARD, US

FIRST AMERICAN IN SPACE

SHEPARD TRAVELED 115 MILES INTO SPACE ON MAY 5, 1961. HE DIDN'T MAKE IT INTO ORBIT THEN, BUT TEN YEARS LATER HE GOT TO WALK ON THE MOON AS PART OF THE APOLLO 14 MISSION.

POP SCIENCE

What was the first sport played on the Moon? Golf! Alan Shepard smuggled a golf club and ball inside his space suit during the Apollo 14 mission. At the end of the day's moonwalk on February 6, 1971, Alan tried to hit two balls just before liftoff. He missed on his first swing but hit the second with his six-iron, propelling the ball a few hundred yards. His space suit was so stiff that he could only swing the club with one hand.

A SPACE-TRAVELING SENATOR

JOHN GLENN, US

FIRST AMERICAN IN ORBIT

A US MARINE AND VETERAN OF TWO WARS, JOHN GLENN ORBITED THE EARTH THREE TIMES IN A 1962 FLIGHT. HE LATER BECAME A US SENATOR. HE RETURNED TO SPACE AGAIN IN 1998, SPENDING NINE DAYS ON THE SPACE SHUTTLE *DISCOVERY*. HE WAS SEVENTY-SEVEN YEARS OLD, MAKING HIM THE WORLD'S OLDEST SPACE TRAVELER.

FROM PARACHUTES TO ROCKETS

VALENTINA TERESHKOVA, SOVIET UNION

FIRST WOMAN IN SPACE

ON JUNE 16, 1963, SHE COMPLETED FORTY-EIGHT ORBITS IN SEVENTY-ONE HOURS ON THE SPACECRAFT *VOSTOK 6*. HER REPUTATION AS AN AMATEUR PARACHUTIST HELPED GET HER ACCEPTED INTO THE COSMONAUT PROGRAM.

HISTORIC COMMAND PILOT

MICHAEL COLLINS, US

PART OF THE FIRST MANNED LUNAR MISSION

NEIL ARMSTRONG AND BUZZ ALDRIN MIGHT BE FAMOUS FOR WALKING ON THE MOON, BUT THEY COULDN'T HAVE DONE IT WITHOUT MICHAEL COLLINS. THE COMMAND PILOT OF *APOLLO 11*, HE CIRCLED THE MOON IN *COLUMBIA*, THE COMMAND MODULE, UNTIL HIS CREW MEMBERS REJOINED HIM. BEFORE HE WENT TO THE MOON, HE WAS COMMAND PILOT OF THE GEMINI 10 MISSION IN 1966.

THE STEPS SEEN AROUND THE WORLD

NEIL ARMSTRONG, US

FIRST TO WALK ON THE MOON

DURING THE APOLLO 11 MISSION, NEIL ARMSTRONG STEPPED OFF THE EAGLE LUNAR MODULE ONTO THE MOON'S SURFACE. BEFORE BECOMING AN ASTRONAUT HE EARNED THREE MEDALS AS A PILOT FIGHTING IN THE KOREAN WAR.

Famous Words

After his historic steps, Neil Armstrong said, "That's one small step for [a] man, one giant leap for mankind." (He skipped the "a" in his statement, but who can blame him? He was walking on the Moon!)

AND THEN CAME BUZZ

BUZZ ALDRIN, US

SECOND TO WALK ON THE MOON

HIS NAME WAS EDWIN BACK IN 1969 WHEN HE
WALKED ON THE MOON, BUT EVERYONE CALLED HIM "BUZZ,"
SO HE OFFICIALLY CHANGED IT YEARS LATER. BEFORE THE FAMOUS
MOON LANDING, ALDRIN PERFORMED A 5 $\frac{1}{2}$-HOUR WALK IN SPACE
DURING THE *GEMINI 12* MISSION. TRAVELING TO THE MOON MIGHT
HAVE BEEN HIS DESTINY—HIS MOTHER'S MAIDEN NAME WAS MOON.

In the Toy Story movies, toy astronaut Buzz Lightyear
is modeled after real astronaut Buzz Aldrin.

POP
CULTURE

A HERO TO GIRLS

SALLY RIDE, US

FIRST AMERICAN WOMAN IN SPACE

SHE ALMOST BECAME A PROFESSIONAL TENNIS PLAYER, BUT SHE
SWITCHED GEARS AND STUDIED ENGLISH AND PHYSICS INSTEAD. NASA
ACCEPTED HER FOR ASTRONAUT TRAINING IN 1979, AND SHE TOOK
HER FIRST SPACE FLIGHT IN 1983 IN *CHALLENGER*. SHE WENT ON TO
START PROGRAMS THAT ENCOURAGE GIRLS TO GO INTO THE FIELDS
OF SCIENCE, MATH, AND TECHNOLOGY.

A STRONG COMPETITOR

GUION BLUFORD, US

FIRST AFRICAN AMERICAN IN SPACE

IN 1978, NASA HELD A CONTEST FOR PEOPLE WHO
WANTED TO BECOME SPACE SHUTTLE ASTRONAUTS. TEN
THOUSAND APPLIED, AND BLUFORD WAS ONE OF THIRTY-
FIVE ACCEPTED. HE SERVED AS A FIGHTER PILOT IN THE AIR
FORCE AND ALSO HAD A DEGREE IN AEROSPACE ENGINEERING.
HE LAUNCHED INTO EARTH'S ORBIT IN *CHALLENGER* IN 1983.

A DREAM COME TRUE

FRANKLIN CHANG-DIAZ, US

FIRST HISPANIC AMERICAN IN SPACE

BORN IN COSTA RICA, CHANG-DIAZ DREAMED OF BEING AN
ASTRONAUT SINCE HE WAS A BOY. HE MADE SEVEN TRIPS INTO
SPACE, AND HELPED TO REPAIR THE ROBOTIC ARM OF THE
INTERNATIONAL SPACE STATION (SEE PAGE 56).

HE GOT THE SCOOP

AKIYAMA TOYOHIRO, JAPAN

FIRST JAPANESE CITIZEN IN SPACE

AKIYAMA, A JOURNALIST, WAS THE FIRST NONPROFESSIONAL
ASTRONAUT TO GO INTO SPACE. THE TOKYO BROADCASTING
SYSTEM PAID MILLIONS OF DOLLARS TO SEND HIM TO THE RUSSIAN
SPACE STATION, *MIR* (SEE PAGE 54). DURING HIS EIGHT-DAY STAY,
HE GAVE LIVE BROADCASTS FROM THE STATION.

SPACE NEEDS DOCTORS, TOO

MAE JEMISON, US

FIRST AFRICAN AMERICAN WOMAN IN SPACE

A MEDICAL DOCTOR, JEMISON WORKED FOR THE PEACE CORPS
BEFORE APPLYING TO NASA. IN 1992, SHE ORBITED EARTH IN THE
SPACE SHUTTLE *ENDEAVOR* FOR MORE THAN A WEEK.

Fallen Heroes

Rocketing off Earth's surface—and landing safely back on the
planet—is a dangerous business. Many people have died in space
or during training missions. Three US astronauts died in a fire
in 1967 while testing the *Apollo I* spacecraft. Cosmonaut Vladimir
Komarov died in 1967 when his orbiting spacecraft tried to land.

The biggest space tragedy occurred in 1986, when the space

shuttle *Challenger* exploded after takeoff. The shuttle carried seven astronauts, including Christa McAuliffe, who would have been the first teacher in space.

In 1984, she filled out an application—along with 10,000 other people—to become the first nonscientist in space. When she was chosen, she planned to give lessons onboard the shuttle that would be broadcast around the world.

"I hope that I can bring that wonder and excitement [about space] back to the students," she said in a TV interview. "I want them to feel that they're part of the space age, because they're the future."

There is a planetarium named after Christa McAuliffe, as well as an asteroid and a crater on the Moon.

POP SCIENCE

Not All Space Travelers Are Human

How do you figure out if it's safe to send humans into space? American and Soviet scientists tested space travel on animals first. Here are some of the most notable critters from the space programs:

Bugging out: The first creatures to be sent into space were . . . fruit flies! In 1947, American scientists sent the flies up in a capsule that traveled 106 miles above Earth, to test the effects of radiation on DNA. They survived the trip. Years later, in 1979, spiders Anita and Arabella were launched to see if they could spin webs in space.

Monkeys: The first simian space traveler was Albert II, a male rhesus monkey. He successfully made it to eighty-three miles up but died when the craft's parachute failed on the way down. Other monkeys have made the trip since and survived.

Dogs: The Soviets sent a dog named Laika, a mutt from the street, into orbit with the *Sputnik 2* satellite in 1957. Sadly, they had no plan to return her safely. They sent other dogs up on future missions, and many of them had happier endings. One cosmonaut dog, Streika, gave birth to six puppies after she returned. One was given to President John F. Kennedy for his kids.

Chimpanzees: In 1961, the US sent a chimp named Ham into space. When he returned healthy, NASA felt it would be safe to send a human in space. And before they sent John Glenn into orbit, NASA sent a chimp named Enos. It was reported that after he landed, he ran around and shook the hands of the crew members.

Other critters: Other nonhuman space travelers include cats, mice, rats, rabbits, fish, jellyfish, amoebas, and algae.

NASA: The Agency Behind It All

In Poptropica, the space program is run by the Poptropica Academy for Space Exploration, or PASE. The US space program is run by NASA, the National Aeronautics and Space Administration. Both agencies have done a great job of getting people (or Poptropicans) into space.

NASA's history began in 1915, when the US Congress established the National Advisory Committee for Aeronautics (NACA). Once the Soviets launched Sputnik in 1957, the US was in a hurry to explore space, so NACA became NASA.

Since then, NASA has sent humans into Earth's orbit and all the way to the Moon; developed the space shuttle, the first rocket-launched vehicle designed for transporting people to and from space; and sent unmanned crafts to explore our solar system . . . and beyond.

NASA OPERATES ITS SPACE PROGRAM OUT OF THE CITY OF CAPE CANAVERAL IN FLORIDA. THE PASE HEADQUARTERS ARE IN CAPE CARPENTER—NAMED AFTER REAL-LIFE ASTRONAUT M. SCOTT CARPENTER.

From Space to You

NASA scientists are constantly inventing things to make space travel easier and safer. Many of those inventions have become products that are useful on Earth, too. Here are just a few:

LIVE ACTION: IF YOU USE A WIRELESS HEADSET TO PLAY YOUR FAVORITE VIDEO GAME OR TALK ON THE PHONE, YOU CAN THANK NASA. THEY CAME UP WITH THE TECHNOLOGY FIRST, AND THEN THE AIRLINE INDUSTRY ADOPTED IT.

A SOFT SLEEP: YOU KNOW THOSE FOAM MATTRESSES THAT EVERYONE SAYS ARE SO COMFORTABLE? THAT FOAM WAS ORIGINALLY DEVELOPED FOR THE SEATS IN SPACE VEHICLES. IT'S ALSO FOUND IN SNEAKERS AND ATHLETIC FOOTWEAR.

FOOD ON THE GO: FOR THE APOLLO 7 MISSION, NASA SCIENTISTS INVENTED A FREEZE-DRIED ICE CREAM FOR ASTRONAUTS TO EAT IN SPACE. IT BECAME POPULAR ON EARTH—YOU MAY EVEN HAVE EATEN "ASTRONAUT ICE CREAM" AT A SCIENCE MUSEUM. OTHER COMPANIES USE THE TECHNOLOGY TO FREEZE-DRY EVERYTHING FROM EGGS AND BACON TO MACARONI AND CHEESE FOR CAMPERS AND HIKERS.

SPORTS SAFETY: IF YOU PLAY SPORTS, YOUR HELMETS AND OTHER PROTECTIVE GEAR ARE LINED WITH THE SAME KIND OF SHOCK-ABSORBENT FOAM DEVELOPED TO PROTECT ASTRONAUTS IN SPACE.

EAR RESPONSIBLE: IF YOU'RE FEELING FEVERISH, YOU MIGHT GET YOUR TEMPERATURE CHECKED WITH A THERMOMETER IN YOUR EAR. THIS IS THE SAME TECHNOLOGY NASA USES TO MEASURE HEAT FROM DISTANT STARS AND PLANETS.

Traveling into space in Poptropica is as easy as hopping aboard a rocket ship. For real-life astronauts, the road to space is paved with hard work, dedication, and challenges.

Getting accepted: Before astronauts begin training, they need to be accepted into NASA. They've got to have a college degree, three years of professional experience, and the ability to meet physical requirements. Anyone shorter than 5 feet, 1.6 inches or taller than 6 feet, 2.5 inches can't get in. Applicants must also undergo a week of personal interviews. If they pass, they become astronaut candidates and begin a training program that's almost two years long.

Flight training: In 2004, the astronaut candidates began training in the T-34, a high-performance training airplane. They learn things such as how to safely parachute from the plane and how to use the ejection seat. After a month they learn how to fly the plane.

Hitting the books: Just like in any school, astronaut candidates go to class, study, and take tests.

Splashdown: Candidates have to train in military water survival and become certified in scuba diving (self-contained underwater breathing apparatus), because it simulates being weightless in space. For part of their swimming test, they have to swim three lengths of a twenty-five-meter pool in a space flight suit and sneakers.

In the wild: Candidates also experience outdoor survival training, learning how to find water, trap animals for food, and build a shelter.

Zero gravity: What's it like to float in a low-gravity environment? Candidates find out when they take a special ride in a padded cargo jet. The pilot flies the jet a certain way to cause weightlessness for the passengers. That makes passengers superqueasy, earning jets like these the nickname "vomit comets."

POP HISTORY

The test director of one of these jets, the "Weightless Wonder," bragged that the crew had cleaned up about 285 gallons of vomit while the jet was commissioned.

Suit up: It's not easy to move around in a space suit, so candidates get lots of practice.

More study: Months of the training are spent learning about and spending time in an actual space shuttle. Candidates also need to study the systems of the International Space Station (ISS).

Language training: Because NASA and the Russian space agency are cooperating to run the International Space Station (along with other countries), candidates must learn to speak Russian before they graduate.

WHEN YOU FINISH AN ISLAND IN POPTROPICA, YOU EARN A MEDAL. GRADUATES OF THE ASTRONAUT-TRAINING PROGRAM EARN A SILVER PIN.

From Asteroids to Supernovas

ASTEROID
Planets Laugh at Their Small Size
An asteroid is a big rocky object that orbits the sun. So is a planet, but what makes asteroids different from planets is mainly their size—asteroids are less than six hundred miles in diameter. (Earth, for example, is 7,926 miles in diameter.)

In our solar system, most asteroids can be found orbiting in a nearly flat ring between Mars and Jupiter. For that reason, it's called the asteroid belt. Asteroids are made of the stuff leftover from when our solar system was formed. The ones in the part of the belt closest to the Sun are made of metals. The ones in the part of the belt furthest from the Sun are more like rocks, and they contain carbon.

Could an Asteroid Destroy Earth?

In March 2013, a congressional panel learned that the chances of an asteroid big enough to destroy a continent or even all of civilization hitting Earth this year are only one in 20,000. Even though most asteroids would be big enough to end life on our planet if they were to hit, none are on a collision course with Earth. If scientists did detect an asteroid on a course to destroy us, it would take five years—and billions of dollars—to develop a way to stop it.

It makes sense that people worry about stuff like this—scientists believe that 65 million years ago, a 6-mile-wide asteroid hit Earth, wiping out the dinosaurs.

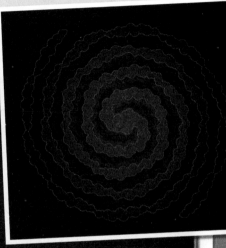

Black Hole
Don't Get Sucked In!

What happens when a really big star explodes? It collapses in on itself, creating intense fields of superstrong gravity. Like a monster with a bottomless stomach, these gravity fields can suck in anything that gets close and tear it to pieces—even planets and stars. When this happens, it's one way a black hole—named because light can't escape from it—is formed.

Scientists have never seen a black hole, but many believe they exist because they've seen evidence of these strong gravitational fields in space. Famous physicist Stephen Hawking has developed many theories about black holes. He says that a black hole will evaporate if it doesn't suck in enough matter to replace the energy it produces. So if the "monster" doesn't eat, it will die.

IF YOU GET SUCKED INTO THE BLACK HOLE IN ASTRO-KNIGHTS ISLAND, YOU WON'T GET LOST FOREVER. YOU'LL JUST GO BACK TO THE PEWTER MOON.

The term "black hole" has become an American expression that people use when they want to describe something that is totally empty of something else. "That fast-food restaurant is a black hole of nutrition," or "My piggy bank has a black hole in it."

COMET

A Giant Snowball with a Tail

Comets can often be seen from Earth without the use of a telescope. They look like bright stars with tails, streaking across the sky.

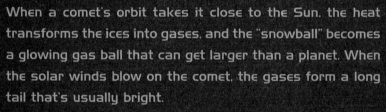

At the heart of every comet is its nucleus, a ball of ice a few miles wide that might have a rocky core—similar to a giant snowball. Like asteroids, they were probably formed from the stuff left over when our solar system was created.

When a comet's orbit takes it close to the Sun, the heat transforms the ices into gases, and the "snowball" becomes a glowing gas ball that can get larger than a planet. When the solar winds blow on the comet, the gases form a long tail that's usually bright.

Some comets take less than two hundred years to orbit the sun, while others can take millions. Humans have been keeping records of comets for centuries, so today's scientists can figure out if the comets in the sky are new ones or if they've been around before.

New comets are usually named after the people who discover them. Sometimes it's named for a scientist, such as British astronomer Edmond Halley, who discovered Halley's Comet. But you don't have to be a scientist to get a comet named after you. In 1996, an amateur astronomer named Yuki Hyakutake spotted a comet through his binoculars. Comet Hyakutake won't come around again for another 14,000 years.

DARK MATTER

You Can't See It, But It's There

You can think of dark matter as one of the ingredients in a galaxy. Scientists in the late twentieth century figured out that the stuff you can see in a galaxy, such as planets and asteroids, only make up about one percent of the galaxy's mass. That's not enough mass to create a gravitational pull strong enough to keep the bodies in a galaxy grouped together—everything would just fly apart.

So they figured out that there must be other stuff, stuff that couldn't be seen, holding the galaxy together. They called it "dark matter" because whatever it is, it doesn't emit or reflect light. As they do with black holes, scientists know dark matter is there by looking at the objects they can see and measuring the gravitational pull around them.

GALAXY

Where Planets and Stars Like to Hang Out

A galaxy is a group of stars, planets, gas clouds, and dust particles that stick together as they move through the universe. Just one galaxy can contain millions, billions, or even trillions of stars—and there are billions of galaxies in the universe!

We live in the Milky Way galaxy, which contains hundreds of billions of stars. These stars revolve around the center of the galaxy, called the nucleus, the same way Earth orbits the sun. Many scientists believe that the nucleus of the Milky Way is a powerful black hole. A massive screen of dust prevents scientists from viewing the center of the galaxy, but radio astronomers get information by reading radio wavelengths. They've dubbed the black hole Sagittarius A*.

Galaxies themselves group together in clusters. The Milky Way is part of a cluster called the Local Group, along with about fifty other galaxies.

GALAXY SHAPES

ELLIPTICAL
- ☑ EGG SHAPED
- ☐ RED CENTER

IRREGULAR GALAXY
- ☑ DOES NOT LOOK LIKE IT HAS A NUCLEUS.
- ☐ COLOR IS BLUER THAN IN OTHER SHAPES.

GALAXY SHAPES

BARRED SPIRAL GALAXY

- ☑ A LINE CROSSES THE NUCLEUS, AND THE "ARMS' SPIRAL OUT FROM EACH END OF THE LINE.
- ☐ THE MILKY WAY IS A BARRED SPIRAL.

SPIRAL GALAXY

- ☑ PINWHEEL SHAPED, WITH THE "ARMS" SPIRALING OUT FROM THE CENTER
- ☐ RED CENTER
- ☑ BLUE ARMS

METEOROID

They Fall to Earth a Lot

This chunk of matter is related to asteroids and comets—in fact, scientists think meteoroids are pieces that have broken off from these objects. Some meteoroids are made of iron and nickel; others are made of stone; and others are made of a combination of stone and metal. Each one can be as large as a house or as small as the period at the end of a sentence.

You might be thinking, "I thought those things were called meteors?" It's normal to be confused. These objects are called meteoroids when they're in space, meteors once they enter Earth's atmosphere, and meteorites when they hit the ground.

Unlike asteroids and comets, meteoroids frequently collide with Earth—about five hundred every year. Most of them have vaporized so much after entering the atmosphere that they are too small to cause a lot of damage. But some can be dangerous. On February 15, 2013, a meteor exploded over Russia, injuring more than one thousand people.

POP SCIENCE

When a meteor hits our atmosphere, it can burst into flames, making it appear as a bright, white flash that streaks across the sky. People used to think these were falling stars or shooting stars.

NEBULA
It Will Make You a Star
A nebula is a huge cloud of gas and dust inside a galaxy. Many of them appear as beautiful colors and shapes, but they all basically contain the same elements: mostly hydrogen atoms with some helium atoms and a scattering of other elements.

Nebulae (plural of nebula) known as *bright nebulae* can be formed in a few different ways. Some nebulae are created from the gas expelled by a dying star. Or if a dying star explodes as a supernova, a nebula can be created from the gas left behind.

And while a star can make a nebula, a nebula can also create a star. This happens in a type of nebula called a *dark nebula*. In a dark nebula, the hydrogen atoms occur as H_2 molecules, which means the two hydrogen atoms are fused together. These packed-together H_2 molecules cause clumps in the dark nebula that cause gravity to collapse—and a star is born.

SOME OF THE MOST FAMOUS NEBULAE ARE NAMED FOR THEIR SHAPES, SUCH AS THE STUNNING CAT'S EYE NEBULA.

PULSAR

A Radio Signal from Aliens?

That's what scientists first thought, because these stars gave off radio waves at regular intervals. Their name comes from the phrase "pulsating radio stars." A pulsar consists mainly of neutrons, is 12 miles in diameter or less, and rapidly spins. It also has a mass 1.35 times greater than the Sun. It is formed by the explosion of a supernova.

QUASAR

A Bright, Powerful Cosmic Mystery

Scientists in the 1960s followed radio signals from the distant universe and discovered bright objects that looked almost like stars. They dubbed them "quasi-stellar radio sources," or *quasars* for short.

They also figured out that quasars are fairly small and really far from Earth, yet they're superbright—one thousand times brighter than any normal galaxy. They also generate huge amounts of power in the form of X-rays, radio waves, and other types of energy.

Today, scientists can't all agree on exactly what quasars are, but many think they are found in the center of some galaxies.

What's With All the Twinkling?

There are billions upon billions of stars in the universe, and probably as many things to learn about them. So here's the short version of what you should know about stars:

* They're made of gas. A star creates radioactive energy, which makes it shine. When this light passes through Earth's atmosphere, it makes the star looks like it's "twinkling."

* They're massive. The radius of our Sun is 430,000 miles, and the Sun and other stars its size are called dwarf stars. Other stars can be much larger.

* They can come in pairs. When two stars orbit around a common point, they are called a binary star.

* There are different kinds of dwarfs. A dwarf star is a star that is average or below average in terms of size, brightness, or mass (like our Sun). A white dwarf is a star that's not very bright and not very large but has a lot of mass. A brown dwarf doesn't have enough mass to be a star, but it still produces some heat and light. A red dwarf star is smaller than our Sun and has less mass, but it burns very slowly so it lasts a long time.

Connect-the-Stars

Ever since humans have been gazing up at the sky, they have imagined that the position of stars in the sky form shapes and pictures. These groups of stars are called constellations. Astronomers use constellations to map the positions of stars. There are eighty-eight constellations, and many still have the names given to them by the ancient Greeks, who imagined them as characters from their myths

Supernova
Some Stars Like to Go Out with a Bang

Stars don't live forever. They're basically big furnaces producing nuclear energy, and most of them eventually run out of fuel and fizzle out. Other times, they violently explode in an event called a supernova. During the explosion, the star becomes millions of times brighter before the pieces of it scatter into space

WHEN A STAR EXPLODES BUT DOESN'T DIE, IT'S CALLED A NOVA. (BUT IT'S PROBABLY STILL PRETTY SUPER TO WATCH, DON'T YOU THINK?)

Astronomy Hall of Fame

In Astro-Knights Island, Mordred studied the stars and planets. These real-world astronomers are just as talented—but definitely not as evil.

Nicolaus Copernicus   1473-1543   **Polish**
He was the first astronomer to propose that the Sun was a "fixed" point in our solar system and that the planets moved around it. He also figured out that Earth moved on its own axis.

Galileo Galilei   1564-1642   **Italian**
This multitalented scientist improved the telescope, which led to discoveries about the surface of the Moon. He also found out that there are more stars in the universe than can be seen with the naked eye.

Johannes Kepler   1571-1630   **German**
He came up with what scientists now call the three laws of planetary motion, which describe the orbits that the planets take around the Sun in our solar system. The Kepler space telescope is named after him (see page 37).

Edmond Halley   1656-1742   **English**
He was the first person to figure out the orbit of a comet

that astronomers had been spotting for centuries. It was named Halley's Comet, and it passes by Earth about every 76 years. (The next visit is expected in 2061.)

Annie Jump Cannon   1863-1941   American
She discovered three hundred stars, but she is most famous for the work she did classifying more than 225,000 of them. She developed a way to measure the light patterns coming from stars to determine their temperature.

Edwin Hubble   1889-1953   American
He established the study of everything outside our Milky Way galaxy. The Hubble Space Telescope was named after him (see page 36).

Stephen Hawking   1942-   British
A brilliant physicist, Hawking became famous for his research on black holes and how the universe was formed. He has been in a wheelchair since the 1960s, after contracting a disease called ALS. He is barely able to move and speaks with the help of a computer, but that hasn't stopped him from writing books about his discoveries.

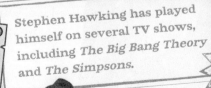

Stephen Hawking has played himself on several TV shows, including *The Big Bang Theory* and *The Simpsons*.

POP CULTURE

They Give Scientists a Closer Look at the Universe

The Hubble Space Telescope (HST)

Earth's atmosphere is great for keeping us alive, but it's a big problem for astronomers. When they observe space from telescopes on Earth, the atmosphere can absorb or distort the light given off by objects in the sky.

How do you solve that problem? By stationing a telescope outside Earth's atmosphere. So NASA built the Hubble, and in 1990, the crew of the space shuttle *Discovery* put it into orbit around Earth.

Hubble's powerful telescope allows us to retrieve information further into the universe than ever. The telescope focuses light from various points and then feeds that light to other instruments. The wide-field camera sends digital images to Earth that become color pictures. If an object in space is hidden by dust or gas, instruments can read infrared light or heat from it. In 2002, the Advanced Camera for Surveys was added to help study the most distant objects in the universe.

Different parts of the Hubble have had to be repaired or replaced over the years, and new instruments have been added. You can't just bring something like the Hubble into the garage for a tune-up, so astronauts do the work in space. NASA plans to replace the Hubble in 2015 with an even more powerful telescope. But the Hubble will go down in history as the tool that changed astronomy forever.

Thanks to Hubble . . .

. . . scientists were able to figure out that the universe is 13.7 billion years old.

. . . we know that a massive black hole is at the center of each galaxy.

. . . scientists were able to observe how new planets are formed.

Kepler

In 2009, NASA launched a new telescope into orbit, Kepler. It's different from the Hubble because it has only one function: to study distant stars and learn if there are any planets orbiting them.

Not even a powerful telescope can pick up an image of a planet so far away, but Kepler looks at a star to see if it blinks in regular intervals. That could mean a planet is orbiting the sun, blocking the light when it passes and causing it to blink. Scientists can study those patterns to determine if a planet exists, its size, its distance from the sun, and whether life, as we know it, could exist there.

BY EARLY 2013, KEPLER HAD DISCOVERED 122 NEW PLANETS IN DISTANT SPACE!

Is There Life Out There?

When you explore space in Poptropica, you'll see many signs of alien life. When you get to the Pewter Moon on Astro-Knights Island, you'll be greeted by friendly green extraterrestrials.

And on the Lunar Colony, there are signs of an ancient alien civilization.

So, does life really exist on other planets or moons? Nobody knows for sure. But

38

remember all of those billions upon billions of stars? Many of them are likely surrounded by planets. It seems strange that Earth would be the only planet in the whole universe with life on it, doesn't it?

Many people are skeptical. If there is life out there, they ask, then why hasn't anyone come to visit us?

Up in the Sky! It's a UFO!

The term "UFO" stands for Unidentified Flying Object. So if you see something in the sky and don't know what it is, it's a UFO. A "flying saucer" is a kind of UFO. It's shaped like a disc and can change direction quickly in the air. *Excalibur,* the flying craft in Astro-Knights Island that takes you to the Pewter Moon, looks like a typical flying saucer.

First Sighting

The term "flying saucer" was coined by a businessman named Kenneth Arnold in 1947. He was flying his small plane near Mount Rainier, Washington, when he saw nine disk-shaped objects flying very fast. He said that they moved like "saucers skipping on water."

Some people say there's a reason why this "flying saucer" story happened in 1947. The first rockets were developed a few years earlier, during World War II, and people became interested in the idea of sending things into space. Others say that the "flying saucers" spotted since then are actually aircraft being tested in secret by the US government.

The band Foo Fighters got their name from World War II pilots who encountered mysterious glowing balls in the air. The phenomenon was dubbed "Foo Fighters," after a cartoon character's saying: "Where there's foo, there's fire."

POP CULTURE

What Happened in Roswell?

If you visit Roswell, New Mexico, today, you can eat at Galactic Sushi, visit the International UFO Museum, or go to a UFO festival. Why are UFOs so popular here? This town was the site of one of the most talked-about UFO cases in history.

It happened in 1947—the same year Kenneth Arnold saw his flying saucers. A rancher discovered the remains of a strange craft that had crashed in his sheep pasture. It was made of a material that the rancher had never seen before. Back then, officials said it was a crashed weather balloon. Fifty years later, the US government said the craft was part of a secret spy project. Despite these claims, people are still convinced that a UFO crashed that day.

Saucers on Film

Some of the best evidence that UFOs might not have been made on this planet come from photos and films taken by eyewitnesses. Sure, there are plenty of fake photos out there, but some of the evidence is hard to ignore.

In 1951, several people in Lubbock, Texas, saw lights flying in V formations over the city. A college student took photos, and one of the witnesses was a college professor. In 1997, thousands of people in Phoenix, Arizona—including the governor of the state—saw strange lights over the city. Many took photos.

While sightings by so many people are rare, new sightings are reported all the time, and more photos and films are recorded. It's possible that there's a reasonable explanation for every single sighting reported. It's also possible that some of them might have an extraterrestrial explanation. But there hasn't been any definitive proof yet.

Are There Aliens Among Us?

While many people have claimed to see UFOs, others have claimed to see extraterrestrials—beings that aren't from our world. Some aliens have reportedly been spotted in crashed UFOs. In the phenomenon known as alien abduction, people claim they were kidnapped by aliens, taken aboard their ships, and then returned.

Little Green Men?

Nobody is exactly sure where the term "little green men," came from, but in the 1950s it was a popular way to describe what aliens might look like. The inhabitants of Poptropica's Pewter Moon fit that category. In reports of alien encounters, however, there have been a few other shapes and sizes reported:

- Humanoids: Some people claim to have met aliens that look like humans. One of the most famous cases is the story of Betty and Barney Hill. One night in 1961, they were driving on a highway when they saw a strange light in the sky and stopped to look at it. As the object came closer, they saw that it was a spaceship with windows, and they could see people inside.

Frightened, they drove away, but they made a wrong turn and the humanoid aliens blocked their path and brought them onto the ship. They were returned to their car hours later, dazed and confused.

- Grays: You've probably seen images of this kind of alien before—bald, with smooth, gray skin; giant, black eyes; and about four feet tall. This type of alien became popular when author Whitley Strieber wrote *Communion*, a book published in 1987 about what he claims was contact with these beings. The book became a best seller, and others came forward and said that they had been abducted by gray aliens as well.

Beyond the Moon

When it comes to space exploration, Earth is just getting started.

Exploring the universe in Poptropica can lead to all kinds of unexplored places. In Astro-Knights Island, you can visit the frozen Ice Planet, the blazing Fire Planet, or the lush Jungle Planet. Humans have imagined fantastic planets in books, TV shows, and movies.

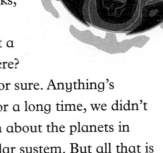

So how do we know there isn't a real Ice Planet out there somewhere?

We don't, for sure. Anything's possible. For a long time, we didn't know much about the planets in our own solar system. But all that is changing.

Space travel takes a long time. Getting from Earth to say, Jupiter, can take more than a year. That's a long round trip for a human to take, and keeping humans alive in space for a long time is expensive. So NASA uses unmanned spacecraft to visit other planets and gather information.

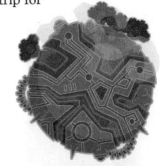

Machines don't need water or

food or oxygen to survive. They can more easily be protected from extreme hot and cold. And they can do the same things humans do, such as take pictures and measure data.

Does that mean humans will never travel beyond the moon? Probably not. But for now, we can explore what's in our solar system—and beyond—from the comfort of our earthly homes.

Mars Exploration Rovers

There Are Robots on Mars! For Real!

Mars is one of Earth's closest neighbors in the solar system. Depending on where we both are in orbit around the Sun, we can get as close as 35 million miles.

Scientists have always wondered whether there was ever life on Mars. They studied Mars with telescopes, but that's as close as they got—until 2004, when NASA sent two robotic vehicles to explore the planet.

The rovers, *Spirit* and *Opportunity*, explored craters that scientists thought might have had water in the past—a key

ingredient for life. They took pictures, collected soil samples, and analyzed the surface to check for any signs of water.

Six years after it touched down, in 2010, *Spirit* stopped sending transmissions. As of 2013, *Opportunity* was still on Mars collecting data.

MARS IS KNOWN AS THE "RED PLANET" BECAUSE, WELL, IT LOOKS RED WHEN YOU SEE IT. THAT RED COLOR IS CAUSED BY IRON OXIDE DUST (ALSO KNOWN AS RUST) ON THE PLANET'S SURFACE. BECAUSE OF ITS COLOR, THE ROMANS NAMED THE PLANET MARS, AFTER THEIR BLOODTHIRSTY GOD OF WAR.

Cassini-Huygens Missions
Piggybacking through the Solar System

Saturn, the sixth planet from the sun, is one of the coolest looking planets in our solar system. Through a telescope, you can see the rings that circle the planet.

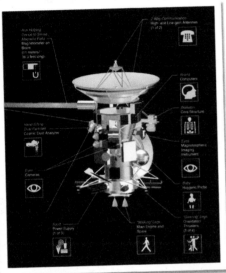

In 1997, NASA got together with the European Space Agency and sent two probes to Saturn. The US probe, *Cassini*, orbits Saturn. The European probe, *Huygens*, broke away from *Cassini* and landed on Titan, one of Saturn's moons.

The mission has resulted in some amazing discoveries. Flying by Earth's Moon, *Cassini* detected water on the surface. In its travels around Saturn, it has discovered six new moons orbiting the planet, and two new rings. Flying by Saturn's moon Enceladus, *Cassini* found geysers of water ice, which could mean that there's a huge ocean under the moon's surface.

Curiosity Mars Rover

Curiosity landed on Mars on August 6, 2012. One of its goals is investigating planetary habitability.

Exploring Jupiter

Scratching the Surface of a Massive Planet

If the solar system were a high school, then Jupiter would be captain of the football team. The planet is larger than all of the other planets combined. It has the most known moons (at least sixty-six). The Romans named the planet after the ruler of their gods.

It's also really popular—seven different space missions have collected data from Jupiter. Most of those missions were flybys. *Cassini* flew past Jupiter on its way to Saturn, and a craft called *New Horizons* passed by on its way to Pluto in 2007. But years before those flybys, scientists got closer to Jupiter than ever before.

Mission: Pioneer

The first craft to fly by Jupiter was the *Pioneer 10* probe in 1973. It discovered that Jupiter has a huge, magnetic tail caused by the planet's magnetic field. *Pioneer 11* journeyed past Jupiter on its way to Saturn in 1974. NASA attached a plaque to each probe with a message (in pictures) for any aliens that might find them.

Mission: Voyager

NASA created two probes for the Voyager mission. *Voyager 2* launched first, on August 20, 1977, and Voyager 1 launched two weeks later. Their mission was to explore the outer planets of our solar system and beyond, and they made some amazing discoveries about Jupiter. Both probes reached Jupiter in 1979 and took more than 33,000 photos between them. *Voyager I* revealed that  Jupiter has rings around it just like Saturn. But the most exciting discovery was found on one of Jupiter's moons, Io. *Voyager I* spotted nine active volcanoes there.

Mission: Galileo

While Pioneer and Voyager provided great information about Jupiter, neither mission spent time in orbit about the planet. Scientists needed a craft that would spend a lot more time there. Named after the astronomer who first spotted Jupiter's moons through a telescope, *Galileo* orbited Jupiter twenty-four times and sent a probe into the planet's atmosphere.

The space shuttle *Atlantis* brought *Galileo* into space in 1989, and it arrived at Jupiter in 1995. Along the way, it flew through the asteroid belt and got the first close-up pictures of an asteroid, Gaspra. It discovered a tiny moon orbiting another asteroid, Ida. When *Galileo* got to Jupiter, it released the probe to take readings of Jupiter's atmosphere.

Galileo went into orbit around Jupiter after that, and stayed there until 2003, when it was sent into the planet's atmosphere to burn up.

To Infinity—and Beyond

The *Voyagers* Keep Going . . . and Going . . .

After getting information about Jupiter, the two *Voyager* crafts went on to study Saturn and its rings. Because the mission was so successful, scientists sent the *Voyagers* even further—to Uranus, then Neptune, and then Pluto, the most distant planet in our solar system. (Well, Pluto is technically a dwarf planet, but it's one of the last planetlike things in our system.)

And the *Voyagers* didn't stop there. They are headed to the outermost edges of our solar system, and when they get there, they'll keep going. As of 2013 they both had reached a section of space called the heliosheath—the last area within reach of the Sun's magnetic fields and solar winds. In a few years they should reach the heliosphere, which is where the influence of the Sun ends and the rest of space begins, somewhere between eight and fourteen billion miles away from the Sun.

Incredibly, the *Voyagers* continue to deliver information to scientists

back on Earth from so far away. That's thanks to the Deep Space Network, a system of space telecommunications centers placed in countries all around the world.

The *Voyagers'* batteries are expected to last until at least 2020. After they run out, the *Voyagers* will continue to drift across the Milky Way, and probably beyond that. In fact, it's possible that they could drift through space for all eternity. Of course, there's always a chance that they will be discovered and picked up by some other species living out there. We may never know.

The Gold Records

Voyager 1 and Voyager 2 each contain a gold-plated copper disc, together with a needle and instructions for how to play the record. If any beings in space discover it and play it, they will hear sounds of nature, 90 minutes of music, 115 pictures of Earth and its creatures (including humans, of course), and greetings in 60 languages.

Living in Space

In Poptropica's Lunar Colony, space explorers and scientists live and work together in a colony built on the Moon. This may sound like science fiction, but many people think that a Moon colony—or at least a small outpost—could exist on the Moon by 2020.

NASA has a plan for keeping astronauts on the Moon for 180 days. Have you ever gone camping in an RV? That's sort of what NASA has in mind with the Lunar Electric Rover. It's a moving vehicle that astronauts could use to explore the Moon's surface, and they would eat, work, and sleep inside it.

Several space agencies around the world are considering plans for a Moon outpost, but a

private company, not a government, might build the first one. Big companies have the enormous amounts of cash that it would take to build a place on the Moon where humans could safely live.

Although no human has ever lived on the Moon, dozens of them have lived in space on space stations placed in Earth's orbit. Years from now they will be known as the first space pioneers.

Can You Cry in Space?

Your eyes can cry in space, but the tears won't fall. You'll just have a big ball of water dangling out of your eye. The more you cry, the bigger the ball will get, but the tears will not roll down your face. You'll need a towel or tissue to mop up the ball of water that forms. (On Earth, gravity helps your tears fall.)

Russia's Space Stations

You Can't Beat the View

The US might have been the first nation to put a human on the Moon, but Soviet Russia was the first to send astronauts in space to live and work. In 1971 they launched *Salyut 1* into orbit. The three-man crew lived on the space station for a record-breaking twenty-three days, but they tragically died when the craft lost air pressure while returning to Earth.

Russia sent up six more Salyut space stations after that, each one an improvement from the last. Some were

occupied by military crews, while others served as scientific labs. The Salyut missions laid the groundwork for the Russians' most advanced space station, Mir.

Mir means "peace" or "world" in Russian. It's a modular space station, which means it's comprised of different pieces, or units. The main, or core, piece was launched in 1986. Five more modules were added, including an astrophysics observatory and a science laboratory.

Between 1986 and 2000, one hundred people from twelve countries (including the US) traveled to Mir via space shuttle. A vehicle named *Progress* transported supplies from Earth to the station. Mir was only supposed to last for five years, so it had exceeded expectations when its equipment started to fail and it was abandoned in 2000. It was sent on a trajectory back to Earth in 2001, which allowed the pieces to fall harmlessly into the Pacific Ocean.

RUSSIAN COSMONAUT AND PHYSICIAN VALERY POLYAKOV HOLDS THE RECORD FOR LIVING THE LONGEST IN SPACE. HE SPENT 438 CONSECUTIVE DAYS ON *MIR*, FROM JANUARY 1994 TO MARCH 1995.

Skylab Is Falling!

In 1973, the US sent up its own space station, Skylab. Astronauts visited during four missions, and NASA hoped to boost it into a higher orbit. But that never happened, and in 1979, NASA announced that the station was going to fall from orbit.

People freaked out at the idea of 100 tons of metal falling from the sky. NASA cleared airspace and tried to direct its fall over the Indian Ocean. Most of the pieces did, although some fell on the small town of Esperance, Australia. Nobody got hurt, but they sent the US a $400 bill for littering.

Millions of pieces of "space junk" are orbiting Earth right now—stuff like parts of satellites and launch vehicles. An average of one piece of garbage falls to Earth each day, although most of it gets burned up in the atmosphere before it hits us.

POP SCIENCE

International Space Station

Bringing the World Together in Orbit

During the space race of the 1960s, the US and the Soviet Union were locked in a bitter Cold War. But the Soviet Union broke up in 1991, and relations between both countries improved. In 1993 NASA and the Russian space agency agreed to combine their separate space station plans, and other countries agreed to contribute, too.

The International Space Station (ISS) is modular, like Mir, and new pieces keep being added. As of 2013, astronauts from fourteen different countries had visited it, and more countries will likely join in.

Partners in the ISS

* Canada
* Japan
* Russia
* United States

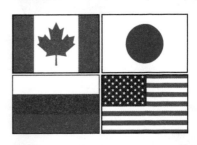

How to Go to the Bathroom on the International Space Station

How do you use the bathroom on the ISS? Sit down and strap yourself in! Once you sit down on the toilet, straps are used to hold your feet against the floor. Bars swing out over your thighs to make sure you remain seated. A tight seal is essential, because this toilet gets flushed with air, not water. If you need to urinate, you have to do it into the hose attachment. It can be used while you're sitting on the toilet or while you're standing up.

Flowing air whisks the human waste away. Solid wastes (poop!) are compressed and stored onboard and removed after landing. Urine is vented out to space. The air is then filtered to remove any odors or bacteria left behind and to keep things smelling good for the next astronaut who has to use the toilet!

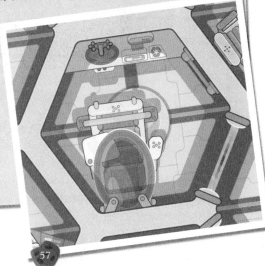

So You Want to Live on the Moon?

Poptropica's Lunar Colony might be a fantasy, but it contains elements that a real-life outpost on the Moon would probably have. Take a look:

* ★ Vehicle bay: Storage for rovers to take inhabitants on excursions on the Moon's surface.
* ★ Barracks: Living quarters for the inhabitants. They would most likely be underground, to shield the inhabitants from solar cosmic radiation.
* ★ Infirmary: An outpost would have to have medical personnel to handle emergencies as well as routine health care.
* ★ Biodome: This sealed environment would replicate Earth's atmosphere inside, creating oxygen and absorbing toxins with plants.

POP SCIENCE

At first, residents of a lunar colony would probably have to eat freeze-dried food that could be stored for a long time. At the University of Australia, they're working on a lunar greenhouse. It would be buried under the soil to protect the plants from harmful cosmic rays, and air containing carbon dioxide from the living quarters would be pumped in to allow photosynthesis. Plants such as lettuce, sweet potatoes, tomatoes, and strawberries could be grown to feed the members of a colony.

* Research lab: Unless the Moon outpost is built for tourists, it would most likely have a lab for scientists conducting research.

A colony on the Moon would probably be built near one of the large deposits of water ice there, so it could be melted down and filtered for drinking water.

POP SCIENCE

Sports in Space?

At first, the main purpose of a lunar colony would be for the inhabitants to study the Moon and perform experiments. But what would colonists do for fun?

Going outside to play would be tough—you'd need a space suit. You'd probably end up reading, playing board or video games, or watching movies.

Scientists have speculated that low-gravity or no-gravity environments could change the way sports are played. Imagine the kind of dunk shot you could make on the low-gravity surface of the Moon? Or how many cartwheels you could do? (Any kind of gym, of course, would have to be built indoors, and probably underground.)

Pop Quiz

1. WOULD YOU TAKE A VACATION ON A SPACE STATION IF YOU COULD?

    A. DEFINITELY.

    B. ONLY IF THERE'S A GIFT SHOP.

    C. NO WAY AM I LEAVING EARTH.

2. WHAT DO YOU THINK ABOUT EXTRATERRESTRIALS?

    A. PEOPLE WHO BELIEVE IN ALIENS ARE SILLY.

    B. YOU NEVER KNOW—THERE'S GOT TO BE SOME TRUTH IN THOSE STORIES.

    C. I CAN'T WAIT FOR ALIENS TO VISIT OUR PLANET.

3. WHAT ROLE WOULD YOU PROBABLY HAVE ON A MOON COLONY?

    A. MEDICAL OFFICER

    B. EXPLORER

    C. SPACE-VEHICLE MECHANIC

    D. SCIENTIFIC RESEARCHER

    E. TOURIST

4. HAVE YOU EVER SEEN SATURN'S RINGS THROUGH A TELESCOPE?

    A. YES

    B. NO

5. WHICH VEHICLE IS THE COOLEST?

    A. MARS EXPLORATION ROVER

    B. LUNAR ELECTRIC ROVER

    C. SPACE PROBE

6. WHICH OF THESE PLACES WOULD YOU VISIT IF YOU COULD?

    A. JUPITER

    B. THE CENTER OF THE MILKY WAY GALAXY

    C. ROSWELL, NEW MEXICO

7. IF YOU COULD GO BACK IN TIME AND INTERVIEW ANY ASTRONAUT, WOULD IT BE . . .

    A. YURI GAGARIN

    B. JOHN GLENN

    C. SALLY RIDE

    D. BUZZ ALDRIN

8. WHICH WOULD BE COOLER?

    A. TO HAVE A COMET NAMED AFTER YOU.

    B. TO HAVE A CONSTELLATION NAMED AFTER YOU.

    C. TO HAVE A PLANET NAMED AFTER YOU.

9. HAVE YOU EVER MADE A WISH ON A STAR?

    A. YES

    B. NO

    C. YES, AND IT CAME TRUE!

10. WHICH OF THESE MYSTERIOUS PHENOMENA WOULD YOU LIKE TO LEARN MORE ABOUT?

    A. BLACK HOLE

    B. DARK MATTER

    C. QUASAR

Index